For Jessie, Katinka & Andrew and all the wonderful kids at Bakewell Junior School - C.H.

For the Pigs in Devon - S.H.

RHINO? WHAT RHINO?

Caryl Hart and **Sarah Horne**

First published in hardback in 2010 by Hodder Children's Books
This paperback edition published in 2011
Text copyright © Caryl Hart 2010
Illustration copyright © Sarah Horne 2010

Hodder Children's Books
338 Euston Road
London, NW1 3BH

Hodder Children's Books Australia
Level 17/207 Kent Street
Sydney, NSW 2000

A catalogue record of this book is available
from the British Library.

ISBN: 978 0 340 98140 5
10 9 8 7 6 5 4 3 2 1

Printed in China

Hodder Children's Books
is a division of Hachette
Children's Books.
An Hachette UK Company

www.hachette.co.uk

RHINO? WHAT RHINO?

Caryl Hart

and

Sarah Horne

Hodder
Children's
Books

A division of Hachette Children's Books

There once was a rhino
who lived at the zoo.
He was lonely and bored,
there was nothing to do.

So early one morning he SQUEEZED through the bars,
And tiptoed away past the slumbering guards.

He ran till he reached a small farm by a lake,
Then came a great rumble that made the ground shake.

"Who ate my lunch?"

Mr Potts shouted out.

And he turned to a pig

with a ring in his snout.

"My dinner has vanished. My pudding's gone too. No one else has come by so it must have been YOU!"

"It's not ME!" oinked the pig as he nosed at the ground. "That rhino just took it while you weren't around."

Away strolled the rhino, now very well fed.

"That pie was delicious
and so was that bread.

Now all I need
    is an outfit to wear.
        I'll just borrow a shirt
            from that line over there."

"Look at
my clothes!"

Aunt Ann cried
in alarm.

And she glared
at a cow walking
down to the farm.

"It's not ME!" mooed the cow with a flick of her ear.

"That rhino came creeping while you were not here."

Aunt Ann looked around but the rhino had gone.

He felt **SO** much smarter with proper clothes on.

"Now all I need
is a place for the night.
I'll sleep in this tree house,
I'm sure it's all right."

"Who wrecked my den?"
little Emily squealed.

And she spotted a sheep
trotting down through the field.

"My toys have been trampled. That bike was brand new. No one else has come by so it must have been YOU!"

"It's not ME!" baaed the sheep, sitting down on a stool.
"That rhino crept up there while you were at school."

That night
while the rhino
was curled up in bed,

The animals met
at the back of the shed.

"You can't go on helping yourself all day long.
Stealing is bad - it's not fair and it's wrong.
You'll have to admit it. You know what to do.
Apologise now or go back to the zoo."

"I beg you," wailed Rhino,
"Don't send me away!

It's no fun being locked
in that cage every day.
I'll write them all letters
and say it was me.
I'll stop being greedy and selfish
- *you'll*
see."

Now the Rhino works hard for his food and his bed.

He no longer steals lunches, but cooks them instead.

He says "please" and "thank you" and "how do you do?"

And he NEVER, NO NEVER
went back to the zoo.